SASHA LANE

THE CATSKILLS:
Waterfall Hikes

MOONHAW

Copyright © 2024 Sasha Lane
All rights reserved
ISBN here: 979-8-9888307-4-0

Trail routes and mileage: Data sourced from AllTrails and Catskill Mountain Keeper
Historical map: Public domain image of the vintage map from NYPL Lionel Pincus and Princess Firyal Map Division
Cover Art: Moonhaw Editorial Team
Photography & graphics: K.E. Knox
Layout and Design: Moonhaw Editorial Team

Printed and bound in the USA
First printing September 2024

Published by Moonhaw Press
PO Box 2301-221
Silverthorne, CO
80498

moonhaw.com

2024

SASHA LANE

the catksills: waterfall hikes

"I can see my rainbow calling me through the misty breeze of my waterfall."

Jimi Hendrix

MOONHAW

FOR MY FOSTER PARENTS AND ALL WHO HELP DOGS IN NEED

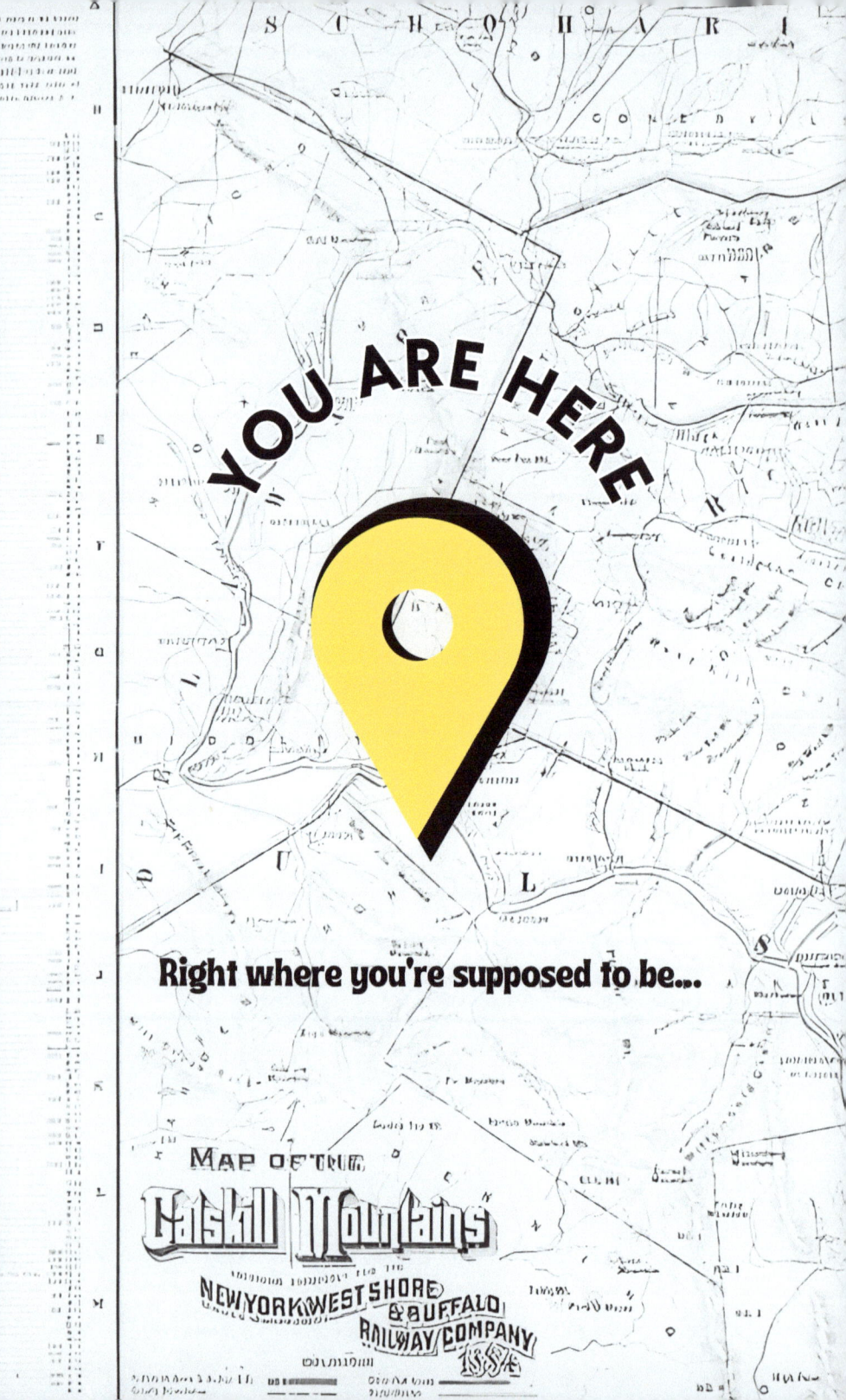

WATERFALLS OF THE CATSKILLS

I
Artist Falls
Round Top

II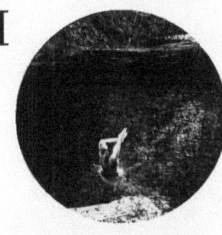
Buttermilk Falls
Denning

III
Diamond Notch Falls
Lexington

IV
Platte Clove Falls
Elka Park

V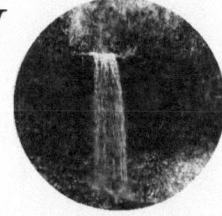
Stony Kill Falls
Kerhonksen

VI
Kaaterskill Falls
Haines Falls

VII
East Kill Falls
Round Top

VIII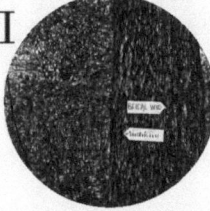
Glen Falls Trio
Round Top

IX
Mine Kill Falls
Gilboa

SAFETY REMINDERS

I
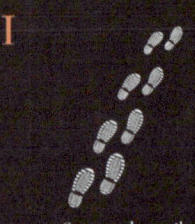
Stay on the trail

II
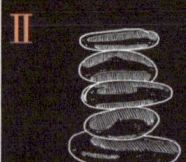
Beware the rocks: spray = slippery

III

Never attempt to climb the waterfalls

IV

Stay away from ledges, especially when taking photos

V

Never wade into fast-moving waters

VI

Wear appropriate shoes that can get wet (no flip-flops!)

VII

Never approach wildlife

VIII

Carry a first aid kit and don't wait to call for help.

Let's keep our waterfalls safe and clean for everyone to enjoy!

vibe check

EACH WATERFALL IS RATED ON A SCALE OF TOURIST TRAP TO LOCAL GEM

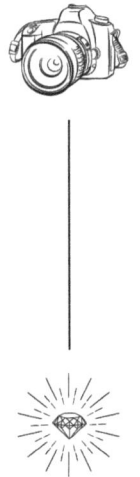

For the human and canine alike, waterfalls are magic, especially in the Catskills. Whether diving into a pool on a sweltering July day or seeking otherwordly solace in mid-January, simply being near one is good for your mental health. Their flow of negative ions and ceaseless beauty have helped define the region as a playground for wellness and wonder for over a century. This non-exhaustive list of dog- and kid-friendly local faves reminds us to explore new plunges or revisit a favorite cascade. Now, lace up those hiking boots and get out into the woods...

ARTIST FALLS

ROUND TOP

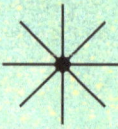

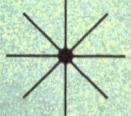

N 42.241

W 74.033

SWIMMING HOLE

VENUS BATH

When: Year-round; there's less access to lower path in winter.

Difficulty: Easy, 2-3 minute walk from the parking lot.

Parking: Small lot across from the Winter Clove Inn's swimming pool. If it's full, follow the paved road to a larger parking lot on the left.

Highlights: Moss, newts, the Alfred Clark Covered Bridge (1976), and a 15 ft-drop into an often swimmable pool. Venus Bath is a bathtub-shaped outcropping in the stream's bedrock created by erosion.

Know before: There are two paths. One takes you to the covered bridge, and the other takes you to the brook below the falls. Keep dogs leashed, and stop by the inn's front desk. The super-friendly staff will give you a map.

visitor vibes

Denning Peekamose Blue Hole

BUTTERMILK FALLS

N 41.924 W 74.414

When: June-September, mornings.

Difficulty: Easy, several hundred feet from the parking.

Parking: Small gravel pullover on the right of Peekamoose Road. No clear signage and room for 6 cars. You can also park in the Peekamoose Mountain lot, a mile west down the road.

Highlights: Steep cascade with a 36-foot drop down a mossy cliff. There are at least 6 more waterfalls along CR-42 as well as access to Blue Hole, a popular swimming spot.

Know Before: Blue Hole is *extremely* crowded. The DEC requires a permit to access the Peekamoose Valley from May-September. Permits can be purchased online at reserveamerica.com.

visitor vibes

N 42.177
W 74.261

POST HIKE, HEAD TO WEST KILL BREWING ON SPRUCETON ROAD FOR A COLD ONE

DIAMOND NOTCH

When: April-October. Virtually no one during weekday mornings. Weekends see a steady flow of hikers.

Difficulty: Easy, 2.2 miles with 300 ft ascent.

Parking: On-site lot at the Spruceton Road trailhead.

Highlights: Side-by-side waterfalls with a 15-foot drop. Large rocks are ideal for hanging out. The trail was first used by the Mohawk to travel between valleys before the Dutch built a road over the pass.

Know Before: For a longer, more challenging ascent, access the falls via the Lanesville trailhead on Route 214. This route is 4 miles with 1,387 ft of elevation gain.

visitor vibes

N 42.130 W 74.087

PLATTE CLOVE

Elka Park

When: May-October from dusk til dawn (Platte Clove Road is a seasonal limited-use highway). Late afternoon/evening after visitors to the 208-acre preserve clear out.

Difficulty: Moderate but very quick ⅓ miles from the road to the base of the falls. Take the trail by the little red house, then stay left. CAUTION: the trail is narrow and descends through a steep, slippery gorge.

Parking: NYSDEC parking lot located off of Platte Clove Road 0.2 miles east of the Preserve (the parking lot is located on the dirt road off the north side of Platte Clove Road). Spots fill up early and cops actively ticket during weekends.

Highlights: 60-foot drop. Short walk from the trailhead.

Know before: Swimming is prohibited. but people do it anyway. Suggested $5 donation to the Platte Clove Preserve. bring cash or donate online at catskillcenter.org/donate.

Bonus fun: Make a day of it in the preserve by hiking the popular Overlook Trail, which links Platte Clove and Overlook Mountain above Woodstock.

visitor vibes

| MINNEWASKA STATE PARK CHARGES AN ENTRY FEE (EMPIRE PASSES ACCEPTED). FOR MORE INFORMATION, PLEASE VISIT PARKS.NY.GOV/PARKS/MINNEWASKA | KERHONKSEN
N 41.734
W 74.295 |

When: March-November (water levels drop to a trickle in summer); 9:00 am to park's closing.

Difficulty: Easy, 1.5 miles out + back.

Parking: Along Shaft 2a Road, in front of the gate. Parking is limited and fills up early.

Highlights: Short hike with great accessibility, plus you can enjoy all Minnewasksa State Park has to offer.

Know before: While a $10 fee or Empire Pass card is required to park at most trailheads in Minnewaska State Park, parking for this trail is free.

Bonus fun: If you cross the creek and scramble up to the top of the falls, you'll find great views and a clothing-optional swimming hole known as the Nudist Pool.

visitor vibes

"Catterskill Falls"

Midst greens and shades the Catterskill leaps,
From cliffs where the wood-flower clings;
All summer he moistens his verdant steeps
With the sweet light spray of the mountain springs;
And he shakes the woods on the mountain side,
When they drip with the rains of autumn-tide.

William Cullen Bryant, 1840

KAATERSKILL

N 42.193   W 74.063

THE ICON
Haines Falls

Muse of the Hudson River School painters

When: Weekdays, winter, sunrise/set. This is the Catskills' most famous falls, so except heavy traffic during the peak season and weekends.

Difficulty: Moderate, 1.4 miles with steep, slick stairs. Cross the bridge and keep right, following the blue-marked trail up the stone stairs to the yellow-marked trail. Stick with this trail until it meets the Middle Pool Spur Trail, a steep series of stone stairs leading the falls' middle pool.

Parking: Laurel House or Scutt Road lots. More parking is available at the Mountain Top Historical Society or North-South Lake Campground. The falls can also be accessed via the Kaaterskill Trolley for $10.

Highlights: NYS' highest cascading waterfall boasts two cascading tiers measuring 260 feet. Thomas Cole painted the falls in 1826.

Know before: You can also view from an observation platform just 0.3 miles from the Laurel House parking area. CAUTION: do not go off-trail or attempt to climb the falls. More than 200 people have died here.

Bonus fun: Add on the 4.4-mile loop to Inspiration Point. This moderately challenging hike has great views and fun boulders for picnicking on. This hike is accessed via the blue-marked Escarpment Trail.

visitor vibes

East Kill Falls

Via Dutcher's Notch

N 42.152 W 74.032

Often-overlooked, this trail abounds with wildlife and traces the old Cairo and East Kill Turnpikes. The East Kill Turnpike, built in 1836, was used by farmers to transport their goods to the Village of Catskill. The hike never reaches a peak and is the longest way to Blackhead Mountain — also the most beautiful.

When: Year-round. The best viewing for the falls is after a large rainstorm - but expect wet feet as the trail turns into a stream.

Difficulty: Moderate, 7.2 miles round trip, 1,424' elevation gain, small bushwack required.

Parking: Small lot at the end of Stork Nest Road off Maple Lawn Road with space for 5 cars.

Highlights: Virtually unknown. Look for deer, bears, and barred owls in colder months.

Know before: The hike begins in a private driveway, so please be respectful. Steep-ish 2-mile climb to Dutcher's Notch (great spot for lunch). From here, the trail levels off. It takes you past a small waterfall that is NOT East Kill Falls. The trail stops 100- 200 feet before the falls. Listen for running water, then bushwack over the East Kill Creek.

Bonus fun: An old homestead sits in a field a few hundred feet west of the falls. They're edible when ripe in late September/early October.

visitor vibes

GLEN FALLS TRIO

N 42.255 ◆ W 74.027

◆ ROUND TOP ◆

When: Year-round, beautiful in winter.

Difficulty: Easy, 2-minute walk from the hotel to the swimming hole at the base of Glen Falls/Bridal Veil Falls. The Icebox Trail is an easy 0.5-mile loop.

Parking: Park at the hotel and introduce yourself at the front desk. Staff will gladly direct you to hiking trails.

Highlights: Three small waterfalls with easy access, no crowds, and two crystal clear swimming holes.

Know before: Trails are accessed via the Glen Falls House, an inn whose grounds are free and open to the public.

Bonus fun: Enjoy a farm-to-table feast at the Glen Falls House's on-site Trotwood Restaurant after your hike. The nearby Biergarten at Mountain Brauhaus is another local legend.

visitor vibes

MINE KILL

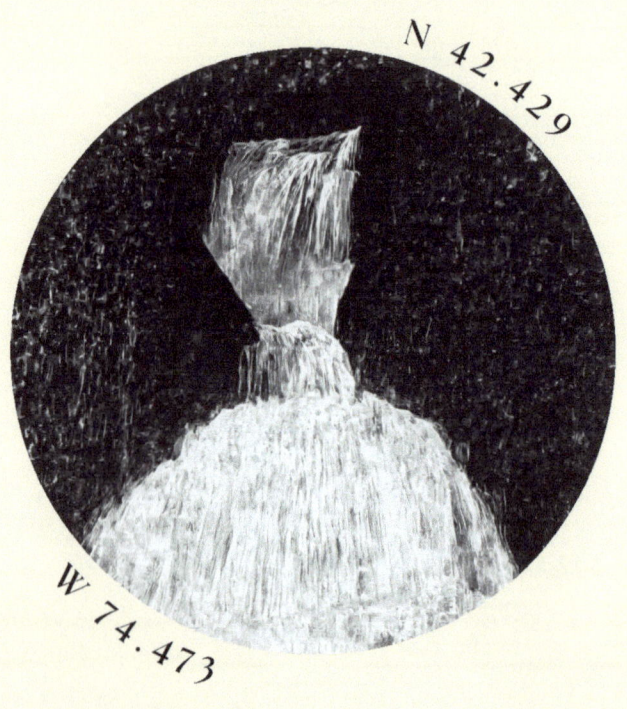

N 42.429

W 74.473

| GILBOA | |

When: Fall or early spring, when foliage is down for a clearer view. Mine Kill State Park is open year-round, dawn to dusk; Pool Complex is open the last Saturday of June to Labor Day, 10am to 6pm.

Difficulty: Moderate, 2.9 miles out + back.

Parking: When you arrive at Mine Kill State Park, park in the small righthand lot marked with a sign that says "Mine Kill Falls Overlook." 1/4 miles south of the park's main entrance, another parking area provides access to the overlook viewing platforms.

Highlights: The scenic Mine Kill State Park overlooks the NY Power Authority's Blenheim-Gilboa Pumped Storage Power Project. The falls boast three-tiered cascades flowing through a narrow gorge with a combined drop of 80 feet.

Know before: 5-10 minute walk from the parking to the viewing platform or take the Long Path hiking trail to the lower falls.

Bonus fun: Mine Kill State Park also has a free Olympic-sized swimming pool and mountain biking trails.

visitor vibes

LEAP AND THE NET WILL APPEAR

John Burroughs

DISCOVERIES

DISCOVERIES

DISCOVERIES

DISCOVERIES

DISCOVERIES

ABOUT THE AUTHOR

SASHA LANE IS A SPIRITED THREE-YEAR-OLD BORDER COLLIE MIX WITH A PASSION FOR EXPLORING THE OUTDOORS. HER GUIDE BOOKS TO THE CATSKILLS OFFER DOG-FRIENDLY TIPS AND INSIGHTS, MAKING EVERY ADVENTURE AS THRILLING AS HER OWN!

www.ingramcontent.com/pod-product-compliance
Lightning Source LLC
Chambersburg PA
CBHW041528090426
42736CB00036B/236